YOUR LIFE

DEVELOPING SKILLS THROUGH LIFE STORY WRITING

NAN MERRICK PHIFER

GLENCOE

McGraw-Hill

New York, New York   Columbus, Ohio   Mission Hills, California   Peoria, Illinois

Photo Credits

Cover, Aaron Haupt; 3b, Catherine Varca; 18, Jeff Greenberg/PhotoEdit; 45, Aaron Haupt; 61, Matt Meadows; 93, Vic Bider/PhotoEdit; 98, Robert Brenner/PhotoEdit, 112, Rich Brommer.

Illustrator

Steve Botts

Writing Your Life—Developing Skills Through Life Story Writing

Send all inquiries to:
Glencoe/McGraw-Hill
936 Eastwind Drive
Westerville, Ohio 43081

ISBN 0-02-803056-7

Printed in the United States of America

1 2 3 4 5 6 7 8 9 POH 00 99 98 97 96 95 94

Table of Contents

Acknowledgments

The author and editorial team wish to gratefully acknowledge the contributions of the following reviewers, whose considerable efforts, suggestions, ideas, and insights helped to make this text a more valuable and viable learning tool.

Debbie Bernhard
ABE/GED Instructor
Lane Community College
Eugene, Oregon

Janie Bonham
Instructor/Adult Education
Paris Junior College
Paris, Texas

Maggie Cunningham
Cooperative Director of
   Adult Education
Schertz, Texas

Steve Flannery
Instructor
Jackson County Center of
   Rogue Community College
Grants Pass, Oregon

Mary Foust
ABE/GED Instructor
Lane County
Eugene, Oregon

Esther Gross
Coordinator of Adult Education
Petit Jean Technical College
Morrilton, Arkansas

Maureen McGory
ABE/GED Instructor
Emerald Job Center
Eugene, Oregon

Lynn Porter
Advisor
Alternative Education
Division of Adult Education
Los Angeles Unified School District
Los Angeles, California

Maxine Rietmann
ABE/GED Instructor
Portland Community College
Portland, Oregon

Vickie Thompson
ABE/GED Instructor
Lane Community College
Eugene, Oregon

Writing Your Life

Introduction

In this book you will use something you really know about to practice writing skills—*your own life!* The book will serve as a guide to some things you can tell about yourself, but you may change those topics or add other ones.

How do you feel about writing? Do you like to write? Why? If not—if you find yourself avoiding writing—you may have had a critic who made harsh comments about your writing at some time. The critic could have been a former teacher, a parent, a friend—or even yourself.

A good critic tells you good points about your writing. He or she also asks questions and tells you what was confusing or unclear. That information is helpful because you can learn from it. But some critics can be very harsh and even unfair in what they say. What does that criticism do to you? Do you "freeze up" because you're afraid that critic is going to say something bad about everything you write?

What many people don't realize is that *you* are your toughest critic. Your critic's voice may stop you at every sentence and say, "No, that's not good" or "You'd better not use that word because you don't know how to spell it." What you need to do is keep that voice quiet so you can *relax* and *write!* Don't worry about details like spelling and punctuation as you write. You can fix those later. Just loosen up and write whatever you want.

As you write about your own experiences and memories, you will also be given some reminders about common errors in English, punctuation, capitalization, and spelling. This information will help you when you are ready to prepare your final copy.

You and your classmates will also serve as good critics to each other by asking questions and pointing out useful things about each other's writing.

Have fun as you write about your own life. When you finish each chapter, file it in a three-ring binder or place it in your Glencoe Portfolio.

You may also any add pictures, drawings, awards, or other accomplishments that you wish. Feel proud of your work!

Earliest Memories

In this book, you are going to develop writing skills by writing the story of your life. You are going to begin with some early memories and answer the questions that appear along the side margin. This is a sample of a practice page.

JUST WRITE

Cross out

Make Changes!

Don't worry about spelling or neatness. You'll make a neat copy later. You'll also check spelling and punctuation then. You may skip or change any paragraphs. Write on the solid lines. Add changes on the dotted lines.

Here is an example of a good, messy practice page.

How was your first name chosen?

I was named Rayman after my mom's
~~father~~ dad but everybody calls me Ray.
My sister calls me ~~Rayman~~

Do you have a middle name?

My middle name is LeRoy. I just
use the "L." LeRoy means "the King"
in French. When Mom was mad she
would yell "Rayman LeRoy!"

What is your last name?

What do you know about your name?

My last name is Williams. I
don't know where it came from.
Coach always called me by my
last name.

Now it's your turn.

Writing Your First Draft:

Just put your ideas on the paper. Answer the questions that appear along the side margin. Whatever you write is all right. Write on the solid lines. Don't worry about spelling or neatness now. You may skip any topic or change it to one of your own choice.

How was your first name chosen?

I was named

_____
_____
_____
_____

Do you have a middle name?

_____
_____
_____
_____

What is your last name?

_____
_____
_____
_____

What do you know about your name?

_____
_____
_____
_____
_____

Word Wisdom

If you write the nationality of your last name, capitalize that word.

Examples:
Spanish, German, Vietnamese, French, Korean, Cuban

Continue Writing!

Remember, you may skip or change any paragraphs.

Sometimes our families tell stories about us as babies.

I was born

When I was a baby

What story do you know about yourself?

Word Wisdom

Capitalize the names of cities, states, and countries.

Examples:
New York, Paris, Chicago, Ohio, California, Alaska, Mexico, China, Nigeria

Keep Writing!

You may skip or change any paragraph.

Who gave you those nicknames?

People sometimes called me by the nickname

Why?

Why is this the right name for you?

Now I like to be called

by my friends.

Why did you like this person?

When I was a child, the person I felt closest

to was

Word Wisdom

Capitalize mother, dad, uncle, grandma only when used like a name.

Examples:
Hi, Mom! Dad and Jason took the bus downtown.

Hint:
If you use words like **my** or **her** or **his** before the word, you don't capitalize it.

Examples:
Aunt Cecilia visited.   I stayed with my aunt.

Keep Writing!

What did you enjoy doing?

When I was a child, I used to

What made you feel good?

Where did you play?

With whom did you play?

 **Word Wisdom** Notice the **d** in use*d* to. Sometimes we don't hear it, but we should write it. Suppose*d* to also has a **d** we don't hear.

Keep Writing!

Remember, skipping paragraphs is OK.

What rules were you supposed to follow?

As a child, I was supposed

How were you supposed to behave?

Tell about a time when you did what you wanted to do.

One time I

Word Wisdom

Should have is the correct way to write these words, but we say them so quickly that they often sound like *should of.*

Listener's Responses

Now that you've written the practice pages of this chapter, you're ready to review your writing. First, you'll **hear** what you wrote. Then, you'll **revise** it.

To hear how your writing sounds, ask a classmate, friend, or teacher to read it out loud to you, or you could read it aloud to a listener. (Tell the reader to ignore spelling and punctuation for now. You'll fix that later.)

☐

Name of reader or listener   Check Box

Next ask your classmate or friend to write responses to the following statements.

1. Describe what you liked about the way this chapter was written.

_____

_____

2. Write a question beginning with *How.*

_____

_____

3. Write a question beginning with *Why.*

_____

_____

4. Please find and underline a sentence you really liked.
   Thank you!

Revising Your Writing:

Consider your listener's responses. You may decide to do any of the following:

- Add information.
- Change words or sentences.
- Rearrange sentences or paragraphs.

Cross out words you want to change. Write revisions on the dotted lines on the practice pages.

Before proofreading, let's review sentence punctuation.

Run-on Sentences

Sentences should be separated by periods when there are no connecting words like **and**, **or**, and **but**.

Examples:

Not this: Desmond wanted to stay home, we watched TV and ate popcorn.

This is good: Desmond wanted to stay home. We watched TV and ate popcorn.
Notice that the second sentence starts with a capital letter.

Separate sentences with periods, question marks, or exclamation marks. Start each new sentence with a capital letter.

Now it's your turn. Rewrite the following sentences correctly.

1. I want my money back, this toy broke the first time we used it.

_____

_____

2. His pickup truck backfired and stopped, he checked all the gauges.

_____

_____

3. We love to dance, we can do country swing, ballroom, and square dancing.

_____

_____

4. Shirley and I went to the beach, we took a bag of sandwiches, the kids came, too.

_____

_____

Hint: Did you discover that three sentences run together in number 4?
You should have written separate sentences.

Check your answers on page 119. Save these tips in your portfolio for future use.

End Punctuation

End punctuation is punctuation that comes at the end of a sentence.

A **period (.)** is used after a statement.

Examples: I have finished the assignment.
I asked her if she would check the files.

A **question mark (?)** is used after a question. (Makes sense!)

Examples: May I have a piece of pie?
What kind of pie do you want?

An **exclamation point (!)** is used to show surprise, emotion, or excitement.

Examples: Look out! Our dinner is on fire!
What a great job you've done!

An order to someone usually ends with a period, but it may end with an exclamation point if you're excited.

Examples: Please read carefully.
Get out of the road!

Now it's your turn. End each sentence with the correct punctuation.

1. Please explain this to her

2. I think she needs to know the truth

3. What a weasel he is

4. Why does he treat her that way

5. Does she know what he is like

6. Do you believe him

7. Get lost

Check the answers on page 119. Save this page for future use.

Chapter 1

You're ready to proofread. Reread your practice paragraphs. Separate any run-on sentences. Check end punctuation. Use the following checklist to complete your final draft. Check the paragraphs you wrote.

1. Did you separate all run-on sentences?
Pry those guys apart.
Then write your initials in the box.

Your Initials

2. Did you use correct end punctuation?
Write your initials in the box.

Your Initials

3. Ask someone to check your spelling.
Don't do it yourself.
We're all blind to our own mistakes.
Ask your proofreader to sign here:

Proofreader's Signature

4. Show your practice paragraphs to your teacher.
Remember: First writing is supposed to be messy.
Ask your teacher to initial the box.

Teacher's Initials

Well Done!

Now you're ready to write your final draft.

Writing Your Final Draft:
Use a word processor in your classroom to write a neat copy of your paragraphs. Double-space and use the spelling checker.

 or

Handwrite a neat copy.
Write on only one side of the paper. Leave wide margins on both sides and on the bottom. Don't skip lines on your final copy. Add photos or drawings if you want.

Put your final copy in your portfolio.

Feel Good About Your Achievement.

CHAPTER

2

Memories of Childhood

In this chapter, you'll write about memories of your childhood.

Writing Your First Draft: Just write! Answer the questions that appear along the side margin. Whatever you write is all right. Write on the solid lines. Don't worry about spelling or neatness now. You may skip any topic or change it to one of your own choice.

Who played this game with you?

A game we used to play was

What did you like about this game?

Where did you get the toy?

My favorite toy was

How did you play with it?

What happened to it?

What made you feel happy?

I felt happy when

What did you pretend?

When I used to play make-believe, I pretended that

Did you do this alone or with someone?

Word Wisdom

Notice the **d** in use**d** to. Sometimes we don't hear it, but it's there.

Continue Writing!

Reminder: You may skip any paragraph.

Where did you do this?

What did you wear?

What things and people scared you when you were a child?

I was scared of

Does your family tell something that happened to you, or that you did or said when you were young?

A story my family tells about me is

How did you react?

My mother (or stepdad, foster mother, or any relative) always used to say

Do you agree?

Punctuation Hint: End a sentence with only one punctuation mark. Informally, we sometimes use rows of marks **!!!!** and combine marks **! ?! ??!**. In formal writing, use just one!

Listener's Responses

Now that you've written the practice pages of this chapter, you're ready to review your writing. First, you'll **hear** what you wrote. Then, you'll **revise** it.

To hear how your writing sounds, ask a classmate, friend, or teacher to read it out loud to you, or you could read it aloud to a listener. (Tell the reader to ignore spelling and punctuation for now. You'll fix that later.)

Name of reader or listener

☐ Check Box

Next ask your classmate or friend to write responses to the following statements.

1. Describe what you liked about the way this chapter was written.

   _____

   _____

2. Write a question beginning with *How.*

   _____

   _____

3. Write a question beginning with *Why.*

   _____

   _____

4. Please find and underline a sentence you really liked.
   Thank you!

Revising Your Writing:
Consider your listener's responses. You may decide to do any of the following:

- Add information.
- Change words or sentences.
- Rearrange sentences or paragraphs.

Cross out words you want to change. Write revisions on the dotted lines on the practice pages.

Before proofreading, let's review what makes a complete sentence.

Incomplete Sentences

An incomplete sentence isn't all there. It doesn't express a complete thought. A listener might say, "Huh?" It may confuse your listeners and readers.

Examples:

Incomplete: Exhausted, sweaty, and thirsty like a long-distance runner.
The listener wonders who or what was exhausted, sweaty, and thirsty like a long-distance runner.

To fix an incomplete sentence, add the missing part.

Complete: After working in the garden all morning, I was exhausted, sweaty, and thirsty, like a long-distance runner.

Incomplete: Whenever we go to the beach to swim.
The listener wonders what happens when we go to the beach.

Complete: Whenever we go to the beach to swim, I get sunburned.
or
Whenever we go to the beach, we swim.
As you can see, there can be many ways to fix incomplete sentences. You have to figure out what the complete thought was.

Now it's your turn. Correct the following incomplete sentences by adding words to make a complete thought. Ask your teacher to check your sentences when you have finished.

1. Thinking of you.

Corrected: _____

2. On top of the house.

Corrected: _____

3. Because he was late.

Corrected: _____

4. Screaming and laughing.

Corrected: _____

Some sample answers appear on page 119. Save these tips in your portfolio for future use.

Proofreading Tip: Follow these steps to check your own paragraphs for incomplete sentences.

1. Read each paragraph aloud backwards starting with the last sentence.
2. Listen to it.
3. Imagine yourself standing on a street corner. A stranger comes up to you and says your sentence. Does it express a complete idea? If it doesn't, add what's needed.
4. Continue reading sentence by sentence from the end of your draft.

These steps really work! Save this page in your portfolio as a reminder.

two, too, and to

Two is a number. You write **two** for 2.

> **Example:**   She has two hands, two feet, two eyes, and—I'm sure—two mouths.

Too has two (2) meanings.

1. It means very, really, or an excessive amount.

> **Examples:**   He drank too much and had to walk home.
> It's too cold in here. Turn on the heat.
> I'd like to buy that truck, but it's too expensive.

2. It means **also**.

> **Examples:**   Maria and Anna will come to our party, and Tony will, too.
> Let's have ice cream, cake, and pie, too.

Now it's your turn. Fill in the blanks with the correct word.

1. Angelo will play the piano and sing _____ .

2. _____ many people crowded into the theater.

3. The show started _____ late. We had to leave.

4. My cycle carries _____ passengers.

5. I want to ride _____ .

6. This recipe calls for _____ cans of pinto beans.

We use the word **to** when we do not mean 2 or excessively or also.

1. It's used to show direction.

> **Example:**   Send the package to her.

2. **To** is also used with verbs to form infinitives.

> **Example:**   I would like to drive.

Check the answers on page 119. Save these tips in your portfolio for future use.

Chapter 2

You're ready to proofread. Reread your practice paragraphs. Separate any run-on sentences. Check end punctuation. Use the following checklist to complete your final draft.

1. Read first for run-on sentences.
Separate them. Check your end punctuation.
Now write your initials in the box.

Your Initials

2. Read from the end to the beginning for incomplete sentences. Fix them.
Write your initials in the box.

Your Initials

3. Check for **too**, **two**, and **to**.
Write your initials in the box.

Your Initials

4. Ask a proofreader to check your spelling.
Ask your proofreader to sign here:

_____
Proofreader's signature

5. Show your corrected practice pages to your teacher. Ask your teacher to initial the box.

Teacher's Initials

Well Done!

Now you're ready to write your final draft.

Writing Your Final Draft:
Use a word processor in your classroom to write a neat copy of your paragraphs. Double-space and use the spelling checker.

or

Handwrite a neat copy.
Write on only one side of the paper. Leave wide margins on both sides and on the bottom. Don't skip lines on your final copy. Add photos or drawings if you want.

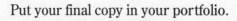

Put your final copy in your portfolio.

Feel Proud About Your Achievement.

Memories of School

In this chapter, you'll write about memories of school.

Writing Your First Draft: Just write! Answer the questions that appear along the side margin. Whatever you write is all right. Write on the solid lines. Don't worry about spelling or neatness now. You may skip any topic or change it to one of your own choice.

How did you get to and from school?

To get from home to school, I

What did you like about this teacher?

My favorite teacher was

What didn't you like about this teacher?

The worst teacher I had was

Word Wisdom

Lots of people use the word *weird* these days. If you write it, notice that it breaks the *i* before *e* except after *c* rule. Weird!

You may change topics or skip them.

What did you enjoy doing? Why?

At school I liked to/My favorite subject was

Why did you like this person?

Someone I liked was/My best friend was

What did you do during recess?

On the playground, I

Word Wisdom

Verbs are the words we use to show actions or existence.

Examples:
She sings well. He is tall. They look happy. Angie cooked dinner.
When we talk about the present, we add an *s* to the verb when it follows he or she.

Examples:
He does. She goes. He runs. She plays ball. He walks to school.

Where did you eat?

At lunch time I _____

What food did you buy or bring?

What happened?

A funny story I remember _____

Why didn't you go to school?

I had to stay home from school when _____

Were you sick?

To make words plural (more than one), we usually add an *s*.

Examples:

Singular	Plural
one quarter	four quarters
one boy	three boys

However, some words change form when they become plural.

Singular	Plural
man	men
child	children
baby	babies
mouse	mice
woman	women

Did you have to take care of someone?

_____

_____

_____

_____

_____

_____

Tell what happened when the weather was bad.

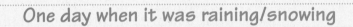
One day when it was raining/snowing

_____

_____

_____

_____

_____

Word Wisdom

Use the **past tense of verbs** when something happened in the past.

Examples:
I _walked_. She _saw_. We _did_. They _went_. He _bought_.

Listener's Responses

Now that you've written the practice pages of this chapter, you're ready to review your writing. First, you'll **hear** what you wrote. Then, you'll **revise** it.

To hear how your writing sounds, ask a classmate, friend, or your teacher to read it out loud to you, or you could read it aloud to a listener. (Tell the reader to ignore spelling and punctuation for now. You'll fix that later.)

_____

Name of reader or listener

☐ Check Box

Next ask your classmate or friend to write responses to the following statements.

1. Describe what you liked about the way this chapter was written.

_____

_____

2. Write a question beginning with *How.*

_____

_____

3. Write a question beginning with *Why.*

_____

_____

4. Please find and underline a sentence you really liked.
Thank you!

Revising Your Writing:

Consider your listener's responses. You may decide to do any of the following:

- Add information.
- Change words or sentences.
- Rearrange sentences or paragraphs.

Cross out words you want to change. Write revisions on the dotted lines on the practice pages.

Before proofreading, let's review some commonly confusing words.

Words That Sound Similar
our and are

Our shows ownership or possession.

Examples: You've got our seats.
Our dog made the mess. Sorry.

Are shows existence or being.

Examples: You are a fine student.
We are waiting while the cook prepares our order.

Now it's your turn.   Fill in the blanks with the correct word.

1. This is _____ tent site. You'll have to move to another one.

2. Where _____ my glasses?

3. You _____ always on my mind.

4. _____ apartment is on the third floor.

5. _____ cows stay in the fenced pasture.

6. I'll show you where they _____ grazing.

Check the answers on page 119. Save these tips in your portfolio for future use.

they're their there

They're means they are.
An apostrophe fills in for the missing letter *a*.

Example: They're (they are) visiting their cousins in Florida.

Their shows ownership.

Examples: Their car was stolen last night.
Karen visited their apartment.
They will show slides of their trip.
Their cows have won ribbons at the state fair.

There is used the rest of the time. It shows location. It's also used with forms of the verb *to be (is, are, was, were, has been, have been)* to show existence.

Examples: Put the package over there. (location)
There is a rattle under the hood. (existence)
There have been many visitors to this museum. (existence)

Now it's your turn. Fill in the blanks with the correct word. Show what you know.

1. I could not find _____ suitcase in the closet.

2. _____ going to be surprised when they receive a bouquet of flowers.

3. Put her paintbrushes over _____ by the ladder.

4. _____ is a law against fishing here.

Check the answers on page 119.

Now make up a sentence for each of the following sound-alikes.

they're _____

their   _____

there   _____

Can you make up one sentence using all three words?

_____

_____

When you have finished, ask your teacher to check your sentences.

Chapter 3

You're ready to proofread. Reread your practice paragraphs. Separate any run-on sentences. Check end punctuation. Use the following checklist to complete your final draft. Check the paragraphs you wrote.

1. Are all sentences separated?
When you are sure, write your initials in the box.

☐ Your Initials

2. Check sentences for completeness.
Read aloud from the last sentence to the first.
Listen. Is each one complete?
When you are sure, write your initials in the box.

☐ Your Initials

3. Check your use of **they're**, **their**, and **there**.
Now write your initials in the box.

☐ Your Initials

4. Ask a proofreader to check your spelling.
Ask your proofreader to sign here:

_____
Proofreader's signature

Well Done!

5. Show your paragraphs and this page to your teacher. Ask your teacher to initial the box.

☐ Teacher's Initials

Now you're ready to write your final draft.

Writing Your Final Draft:
Use a word processor in your classroom to write a neat copy of your paragraphs. Double-space and use the spelling checker. Add photos or drawings if you want.

 or

Handwrite a neat copy. Write on only one side of the paper. Leave wide margins on both sides and on the bottom. Don't skip lines on your final copy. You may write around any photos or drawings, too.

Put your final copy in your portfolio.

Feel Pleased With Your Achievement.

CHAPTER 4

Childhood Dreams

In this chapter, you'll write about your childhood dreams.

Writing Your First Draft:

Just write! Answer the questions that appear along the side margin. Whatever you write is all right. Write on the solid lines. Don't worry about spelling or neatness now. You may skip any topic or change it to one of your own choice.

What did you like to do or have to do on Saturdays?

On Saturdays I

Did your family do something together?

On Sundays we

What did you long to do, or to have, or to become?

I daydreamed about

Word Wisdom Capitalize days of the week: Saturday, Wednesday, Friday. Also capitalize months: March, May, December.

You may change topics.

What activity or job did you hate to do?

I didn't like

How did this person act?

A relative (or neighbor) I especially remember

What did you like or dislike about this person?

I didn't like

Reminder: Capitalize **aunt, uncle,** and **grandparents** when they're used like a name—Uncle Bud and Grandma Rose—but not when saying **my** uncle or **our** grandmother.

Remember, skipping paragraphs is OK.

What was your favorite meal?

My favorite meal was

How were these foods fixed?

Foods my family used to eat were

Which were your favorites?

Did you dislike any?

Word Wisdom If you write about eating a piece of something, spell **piece** with the *i* before *e*.

What did you dream of becoming,

I wished I could

or having,

or doing?

When did you feel secure?

I felt safe and happy when

I wished I could

What was your favorite season?

My favorite season was

What did you do with friends?

I/we used to

What did you do with your family?

What did you do when you were alone?

Seasons are not capitalized: fall, winter, spring, summer.

Did you have a pet?

Tell about it.

Did you care for farm animals?

What was it like?

An animal I remember was

_____

_____

_____

_____

_____

Where did you go?

Who were you with?

How long were you there?

I remember going

_____

_____

_____

_____

Where was it?

What was it like?

Did you feel safe there?

What did you do there?

My special or favorite place was

_____

_____

_____

_____

If you would like to write more, add your own paper to these pages.

Now that you've written the practice pages of this chapter, you're ready to review your writing. First, you'll **hear** what you wrote. Then, you'll **revise** it.

To hear how your writing sounds, ask a classmate, friend, or teacher to read it out loud to you, or you could read it aloud to a listener. (Tell the reader to ignore spelling and punctuation for now. You'll fix that later.)

☐
Check Box

_____
Name of reader or listener

Next ask your classmate or friend to write responses to the following statements.

1. Describe what you liked about the way this chapter was written.

_____

_____

2. Write a question beginning with *How.*

_____

_____

3. Write a question beginning with *Why.*

_____

_____

4. Please find and underline a sentence you really liked.
Thank you!

Revising Your Writing:

Consider your listener's responses. You may decide to do any of the following:

- Add information.
- Change words or sentences.
- Rearrange sentences or paragraphs.

Cross out words you want to change. Write revisions on the dotted lines on the practice pages.

Before proofreading, let's find out about apostrophes.

Apostrophes

Apostrophes look like high-flying commas.

Example: Here's one.   ,

Apostrophes have two basic uses.

1. They show where a letter is missing.

Examples: The apostrophe shows where the *o* is missing.   do n**o**t ------ don't

Here the *a* is missing.   we *a*re ------ we're

    I *a*m ------ I'm

What letter is missing here? _____   there is ------ there's

2. An apostrophe can show ownership.

Examples:

Tyrone's car	Tyrone owns the car.
Tondra's secret	The secret is Tondra's.
The church's steeple	The steeple belongs to the church.

Now it's your turn. Give an example of each use of apostrophes. Ask your teacher to check your sentences when you have finished.

_____

_____

_____

_____

_____

_____

_____

Sometimes people who haven't learned these rules put an apostrophe before every final **s**. Remember, use apostrophes to show where a letter is missing or to show ownership.

Check the sample answers on page 119. Save these tips in your portfolio for future use.

Apostrophes

Now you know that the apostrophe in the following example is a mistake.

Example: Ali slide's to home base.

No letter is missing. *Slide's* should not have an apostrophe. The word *slides* doesn't show ownership.

Here's another mistake.

Example: The girl's are going with us.

You explain why *girl's* doesn't need an apostrophe.

_____

_____

Now it's your turn. Rewrite the following sentences correctly.

1. Louis wont listen to me.

_____

2. Thats my bus pass.

_____

3. Sallys dog bit someone.

_____

4. The girls laughed and laughed.

_____

5. Tiwana rides horses.

_____

The last two sentences don't need apostrophes. However, the first three do. Can you explain why?

_____

_____

_____

Check the answers on page 119. Save these tips in your portfolio for future use.

you're and your
it's and its

You're means you are. The apostrophe fills in for the missing *a*.

Example: You're (you are) my friend.

Your shows ownership.

Example: This is your wallet. Where are your keys?

Now it's your turn.   Fill in the blanks with the correct words.

1. _____ going to be late for class!

2. I enjoyed looking at _____ vacation photos.

3. Here's _____ headphone.

4. _____ sitting in the first row of the theater.

Pretty easy, huh?

Now make up a sentence using **you're**. Ask your teacher to check your sentence when you have finished.

_____

_____

_____

And don't forget making up a sentence using **your**.

_____

_____

_____

It's means it is or it has (been). The apostrophe fills in for the missing letter *i* or the missing letters *ha*.

> **Examples:** I wonder if it's (it is) too early.　　　It's (it has) been a long day.

Its—with no apostrophe—shows ownership.

> **Examples:** The horse flicked its tail.
> The house lost its roof in the tornado.

Now it's your turn. Fill in the blanks with the correct words.

5. The cat licked _____ paw.

6. _____ been difficult, but we made it!

7. I think _____ a good idea, don't you?

8. I need to fix this shoe. _____ heel is broken.

Now let's mix them up.

9. Haven't you made up _____ mind yet?

10. _____ taking a long time!

11. What are _____ concerns about the project?

12. Let's list _____ advantages.

Check the answers on page 119. Save these tips in your portfolio for future use.

Chapter 4

You're ready to proofread. Reread your practice paragraphs. Separate any run-on sentences. Check end punctuation. Use the following checklist to complete your final draft.

1. Check each paragraph for run-on sentences. Separate any you find. When you are finished, write your initials in the box.

Your Initials

2. Read aloud from the last sentence to the first. Listen for incomplete sentences. Then correct any you find. When you are finished, write your initials in the box.

Your Initials

3. Did you choose the correct spelling of **they're**, **their**, or **there**? **Your** or **you're**? **It's** or **its**? If you did, then initial the box.

Your Initials

4. You've already checked apostrophes. Wow! Look how much you already know! Initial the box.

Your Initials

5. Ask a proofreader to check your spelling. Ask your proofreader to sign here:

_____
Proofreader's signature

6. Ask your teacher to check your work. Ask your teacher to initial the box.

Teacher's Initials

Good for You!

Now you're ready to write your final draft.

Writing Your Final Draft: Use a word processor in your classroom to write a neat copy of your paragraphs. Double-space and use the spelling checker.

or

Handwrite a neat copy. Write on only one side of the paper. Leave wide margins on both sides and on the bottom. Don't skip lines on your final copy. Add photos or drawings if you want. You may write around any photos or drawings, too.

Put your final copy
in your portfolio.

You've Written Four Chapters!

CHAPTER

5

Teen Dreams

In this chapter, you'll write about dreams you had when you were a teenager.

Writing Your First Draft: Just write! Answer the questions that appear along the side margin. Whatever you write is all right. Write on the solid lines. Don't worry about spelling or neatness now. You may skip any topic or change it to one of your own choice.

What styles were "in" at school?

At school we wore

What type of shoes?

What kinds of pants?

What did you do to your hair to style it?

To fix my hair I would

What did you like about your body?

I felt my body was

What did you think was wrong with it?

Who made you feel that way?

Word Wisdom

Use commas to separate items in a list.

Examples:
I washed my hair, combed it, dried it, and styled it.
Put a comma after every item before the *and*.

Keep Writing!

Who was someone you liked?

I liked _____ because _____

Why did you like this person?

We used to

When you were together what did you do?

Capitalize brand names.

For snacks I liked to buy

Use quotation marks ("_____") around names of songs.

My favorite songs from my teen years were

Word Wisdom Capitalize the first word and other important words in titles of books, short stories, plays, songs, poems, movies, and TV shows.

Examples:
The House on Mango Street
"I Heard It Through the Grapevine"
"Ode to a Nightingale"

You may change or skip any paragraph.

Tell about chores or a job you had, or brothers and sisters you took care of.

What did you do?

What was good or bad about this responsibility?

A responsibility I had was

_____

_____

_____

_____

_____

What advice or praise or scolding did you receive?

My family would tell me to

_____

_____

What did you want to do, to be, to become?

I dreamed of

_____

_____

_____

_____

Put the words that people actually say in quotation marks. Separate them from the speaker's words with a comma, question mark, or exclamation point.

Examples:
Ty yelled, "Look out!"
"You did a good job," said Aunt Trish.
"May I help you?" she asked.

Listener's Responses

Now that you've written the practice pages of this chapter, you're ready to review your writing. First, you'll **hear** what you wrote. Then, you'll **revise** it.

To hear how your writing sounds, ask a classmate, friend, or teacher to read it out loud to you, or you could read it aloud to a listener. (Tell the reader to ignore spelling and punctuation for now. You'll fix that later.)

_____   ☐
Name of reader or listener   Check Box

Next ask your classmate or friend to write responses to the following statements.

1. Describe what you liked about the way this chapter was written.

_____

_____

2. Write a question beginning with *How.*

_____

_____

3. Write a question beginning with *Why.*

_____

_____

4. Please find and underline a sentence you really liked.
   Thank you!

Revising Your Writing:
Consider your listener's responses. You may decide to do any of the following:

- Add information.
- Change words or sentences.
- Rearrange sentences or paragraphs.

Cross out words you want to change. Write revisions on the dotted lines on the practice pages.

Before proofreading, let's review some commonly confusing words.

Homonyms
threw and through

Threw means tossed or pitched.

Examples: I threw a stick for my dog.
Sammy threw my love letter into the wastebasket.

Through spells the other meanings: into, between, finished, and other meanings different from tossed.

Examples: We walked through the gate.   (between)
Bonita is through with her chores.   (finished)

Now it's your turn. Fill in the blanks with the correct words.

1. The youngest child _____ a purse out the window.

2. I'll stay with you _____ thick and thin.

3. Aren't you _____ washing those dishes yet?

4. We'll be driving _____ a long, dark tunnel.

5. Monica _____ the basketball.

6. It went _____ the basket, and she scored for her team.

Check the answers on page 119. Save these tips in your portfolio for future use.

In your own words, explain the rule.

_____

_____

Make up your own sentence for each word.

_____

_____

Ask a friend to check your rules and sentences. Save this page in your portfolio for future use.

quit quiet quite

Quit means stop. Look at the last two letters—*it*.

Examples: Quit it!   He plans to quit his job.

Quiet means silent. Look at the last two letters—*et*. The spelling says qui*et*.

Examples: The librarian asked the students to be quiet. "Quiet, please."

Quite means very. The *i* says *eye*—"qu *eye* t."

Examples: You are quite something. This is not quite what I wanted.

Now it's your turn. Fill in the blanks with the correct words.

1. Turn off that boombox and be _____ .

2. Josie will _____ her job when school starts.

3. Dave is _____ broad through the shoulders.

4. That's _____ all right.

5. Sarah and Kate found a _____ little restaurant.

6. _____ poking me!

7. The movie will begin _____ early, so be ready.

8. I _____ smoking and feel much better.

9. He's a day sleeper, so please be _____ .

10. I hope these words are _____ easy for you now.

Check the answers on page 119. Save these tips in your portfolio for future use.

Let's **quit quite quietly** and go on to the next page.

than and then

Than is used for making comparisons.

Examples:

BIGGER THAN

Louder than

Smaller than

Better than

Worse than

Then is used the rest of the time. **Then** shows time or the passage of time.

Examples: Wait until dark. Then we'll go to the fair.
When you pay the parking fee, then I'll open the gate.

Now it's your turn. Fill in the blanks with the correct words.

1. I'm smarter _____ you are.

2. Wash the car first. _____ I'll give you a ride.

3. My cake tastes sweeter _____ yours.

4. Alfred waited until he saw the monster's face, and _____
he turned and ran.

5. My brother likes swimming better _____ jogging.

6. First we'll buy vegetables, and _____ we'll make
a stirfry.

Check the answers on page 119.

Now make up a sentence for each word. Ask your teacher to check your sentences
when you have finished.

_____

_____

Save these tips in your portfolio for future use.

Chapter 5

Now reread your practice paragraphs. Separate any run-on sentences. Use the following checklist to complete your final draft.

1. Check your use of apostrophes. Did you use apostrophes only to show where letters are missing or to show ownership? If you did, write your initials in the box.

Your Initials

2. Check your sentences to be sure they're not run-on or incomplete. When you're finished, write your initials in the box.

Your Initials

3. Did you choose the correct spelling for **threw** or **through**? **Quit**, **quite**, or **quiet**? When you're finished, write your initials in the box.

Your Initials

4. Ask a proofreader to check your spelling. Ask your proofreader to sign this line.

Proofreader's signature

5. Show your work to your teacher. Ask your teacher to initial the box.

Teacher's Initials

Well Done!

Now you're ready to write your final draft.

Writing Your Final Draft:
Use a word processor in your classroom to write a neat copy of your paragraphs. Double-space and use the spelling checker. Add photos or drawings if you want.

 or

Handwrite a neat copy. Write on only one side of the paper. Leave wide margins on both sides and on the bottom. Don't skip lines on your final copy. Write around them. Put your final copy in your portfolio.

Pat Yourself on the Back!

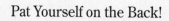

Tell Someone About Your Achievement.

CHAPTER 6

Dreams of Entering Adulthood

In this chapter, you'll write about your dreams of adulthood.

Writing Your First Draft: Just put your ideas on the paper. Answer the questions that appear along the side margin. Whatever you write is all right. Write on the solid lines. Don't worry about spelling or neatness now. You may skip any topic or change it to one of your own choice.

Describe what you wanted.

I saved my money to buy

How long did you save?

Did you get it?

Keep Writing!

What did you like to make, or play, or do?

How did you get started?

Something I liked to do was

What did you do together?

What did you enjoy about this person?

A friend I remember/still have is

What did you do?

Did you live on your own?

Did you do things your parents didn't want you to do?

I showed my independence by

Did you play or watch?

Where were you?

How did you get interested?

The sport I liked best was

Can you name songs or musicians?

My favorite kind of music was

What did you like about them?

Would you play an instrument?

If I could be on stage, I'd like to

Would you sing?

Would you act?

Would you dance?

Do you remember their names?

My favorite movies/TV shows were

Who were the stars?

Why did you like them?

Where did you see them?

Use quotation marks around the titles of shorter works—poems, songs, short stories, or TV shows. Underline (or use italics on a word processor) titles of longer works—books, plays, or movies.

Examples:
Beloved (novel)
"Rules of the Game" (short story)
Dances with Wolves (movie)
"Let It Be" (song)

Listener's Responses

Now that you've written the practice pages of this chapter, you're ready to review your writing. First, you'll **hear** what you wrote. Then, you'll **revise** it.

To hear how your writing sounds, ask a classmate, friend, or teacher to read it out loud to you, or you could read it aloud to a listener. (Tell the reader to ignore spelling and punctuation for now. You'll fix that later.)

☐ Check Box

Name of reader or listener _____

Next ask your classmate or friend to write responses to the following statements.

1. Describe what you liked about the way this chapter was written.

_____

_____

2. Write a question beginning with *How.*

_____

_____

3. Write a question beginning with *Why.*

_____

_____

4. Please find and underline a sentence you really liked.
Thank you!

Revising Your Writing:

Consider your listener's responses. You may decide to do any of the following:

- Add information.
- Change words or sentences.
- Rearrange sentences or paragraphs.

Cross out words you want to change. Write revisions on the dotted lines on the practice pages.

Before proofreading, let's review some more homonyms.

More Homonyms (Sound-Alikes)
bye buy by

Let's start with the easiest. **Bye.**
Bye is short for good-bye.

Examples: The baby waved bye-bye.   Sometimes it is hard to say good-bye.

Buy means to purchase.

Example: He went to the store to buy chocolate yogurt.

By indicates location, nearness, and relationship.

Examples: Come sit by me.
By the way, we walked by your place.
This song was written by an unknown composer.

Now it's your turn.   See if you got it. Fill in the blanks with the correct words.

1. Let's drive _____ Ronnie's Market.

2. I want to _____ some corn.

3. We need to have dinner ready _____ 6 P.M.

4. Have a good trip, _____ !

5. These answers were written _____ me.

Check the answers on page 119. Keep this page in your portfolio for future use.

Now check your paragraphs for your use of **bye, buy,** and **by.**

An Important Review

To complete these exercises, it's OK to look back at your Tips and Pointers.

Rewrite this run-on sentence. Ask your teacher to check your sentence when you are finished.

We were sitting in the balcony, I heard him start to laugh.

_____

_____

Fix this incomplete sentence.

Waiting to see what would happen next.

_____

_____

Put apostrophes in the words that need them. If the sentence is correct, mark it with a C for correct.

1. Im going to school at night.

2. Dont do that!

3. Thats Garys jacket.

4. I swatted ten flies.

   Hint: Did you put two apostrophes in sentence 3, for two different reasons?

   Did you leave sentence 4 without apostrophes since the word _flies_ is just plural?

Underline the correct word in each sentence.

5. (Your/You're) almost done now.

6. (Your/You're) writing has improved.

7. (There/They're/Their) great!

8. (Its/It's) been hard work.

You just polished your tips and pointers.

Check your answers on pages 119–120.

Chapter 6

Reread your practice paragraphs. Using the following checklist, complete your final draft.

1. Are your sentences separated?
Separate any run-on sentences.
Write your initials in the box.

Your Initials

2. Is each sentence complete?
Listen, from last to first.
When each one is all there,
write your initials in the box.

Your Initials

3. Did you check sound-alikes?
Did you check the correct
spelling of these words?
Write your initials in the box.

Your Initials

4. Ask a proofreader to check your spelling.
Thank your proofreader. Ask your
proofreader to sign this line.

_____
Proofreader's signature

Well Done!

5. Show your paragraphs to your teacher.
Ask your teacher to initial the box.

Teacher's Initials

Now you're ready to write your final draft.

You've made a lot of progress!

Writing Your Final Draft:
Use a word processor in your classroom to write a neat copy of your paragraphs. Double-space and use the spelling checker. Add photos, drawings, or souvenirs from scrapbooks if you want.

or

Handwrite a neat copy. Write on only one side of the paper. Leave wide margins on both sides and on the bottom. Don't skip lines on your final copy. Put your final copy in your portfolio.

Feel Terrific About Your Achievement!

Memories of Frights and Thrills

In this chapter, you'll write about what scared or upset you, and the people you liked and trusted.

Writing Your First Draft: Just write! Answer the questions that appear along the side margin. Whatever you write is all right. Write on the solid lines. Don't worry about spelling or neatness now. You may skip any topic or change it to one of your own choice.

Did you ride a bus or train, or did you have a truck or car or cycle?

I used to ride

When did your heart beat with fear?

A time when I felt frightened was when

What happened?

What did frighten you?

I was really afraid of

Keep Writing!

What do you like about the one you chose?

If I could have any car, bike, or truck, I'd

choose

What color do you like?

What features would it have?

What did you find to do?

For fun I

Word Wisdom   **Choose** rhymes with *use* and *news*.
Chose rhymes with *hose* and *nose* and *toes*. It is the past tense of *choose*.

Keep Writing!

Remember that skipping paragraphs is OK.

Were your feelings hurt or were you injured?

I was hurt one time when

How old were you?

What were you doing?

What happened?

Was anyone else hurt?

Keep Writing!

You may change any paragraph topic or skip it.

We've all felt low at times.

I felt low when

Whom did you trust?

A person who made me feel safe was/is

Why?

Word Wisdom

If you use the word depressed, write one *p* and double the *s*.
If you use the word disappointed, write one *s* and double the *p*.
If you use the word coming, write only one *m*.

Listener's Responses

Now that you've written the practice pages of this chapter, you're ready to review your writing. First, you'll **hear** what you wrote. Then, you'll **revise** it.

To hear how your writing sounds, ask a classmate, friend, or teacher to read it out loud to you, or you could read it aloud to a listener. (Tell the reader to ignore spelling and punctuation for now. You'll fix that later.)

_____

Name of reader or listener   Check Box ☐

Next ask your classmate or friend to write responses to the following statements.

> **1.** Describe what you liked about the way this chapter was written.
>
> _____
>
> _____
>
> **2.** Write a question beginning with *How.*
>
> _____
>
> _____
>
> **3.** Write a question beginning with *Why.*
>
> _____
>
> _____
>
> **4.** Please find and underline a sentence you really liked.
>   Thank you!

Revising Your Writing:

Consider your listener's responses. You may decide to do any of the following:

- Add information.
- Change words or sentences.
- Rearrange sentences or paragraphs.

Cross out words you want to change. Write revisions on the dotted lines on the practice pages.

Before proofreading, let's review some more homonyms (sound-alikes).

Sneaky Sound-Alikes: break and brake

Break is about coming apart.

Examples: This fragile glass is sure to break.
Let's take a break from our work.
I hope he'll break that nasty habit.

A **brake** is on a car or other machine. It slows the moving parts.

Examples: There's a stop sign. Hit the brake!
These brakes should be relined by a mechanic.

Now it's your turn. Fill in the blanks with the correct words.

1. When the engineer pulled a lever, the _____ squealed.

2. I'll _____ my nails if I scrub pans. You wash them.

3. Carla is trying to _____ up their romance.

4. I wish my skates had a _____ .

Check the answers on page 120.

In your own words, restate the meaning of each word. Then write a sentence using each word.

Break _____

_____

Brake _____

_____

Ask your teacher to check these sentences.

Save these tips in your portfolio for future use.

More Sneaky Sound-Alikes: whole and hole

A **hole** is a pit, hollow, or gap.

> **Example:** The mole dug a hole and disappeared down it.

A **whole** means the entire thing.

> **Example:** We ate the whole pizza. Yummmmmmmmmmmmmmmmmmmmm.

Now it's your turn. Fill in the blanks with the correct words.

1. Don't cut the apple in half. I want a _____ one.

2. You have a _____ in the seat of your pants.

Check the answers on page 120.

Time for a Little Review of Won't and Want

Won't has an apostrophe where the o is missing.
Want doesn't need an apostrophe because nothing is missing.

Add apostrophes if they are needed in these sentences.

3. I want a thick slice of hot bread.

4. You wont like what I'm about to say.

Now you make up sentences using *won't* and *want.*

_____

_____

Ask your teacher to check your sentences when you are finished.

Save this page in your portfolio.

Chapter 7

Reread your practice paragraphs. Use the following checklist to complete your final draft.

1. Reread your paragraphs for run-on sentences. Separate any you find. Write your initials in the box.

☐
Your Initials

2. Read your paragraphs aloud from end to beginning, listening for incomplete sentences. Fix them and write your initials in the box.

☐
Your Initials

3. If you found and fixed any sneaky sound-alikes, put a + for good work in the box.

☐
Your Initials

4. Ask a proofreader to check spellings. Get your proofreader's signature here.

_____
Proofreader's signature

5. Ask your teacher to check your work. Ask your teacher to initial the box.

☐
Teacher's Initials

Well Done!

Now you're ready to write your final draft.

Writing Your Final Draft:
Using a word processor in your classroom, write a neat copy of your paragraphs. Double-space and use the spelling checker. Add photos or drawings if you want.

or

Handwrite a neat copy. Write on only one side of the paper. Leave wide margins on both sides and on the bottom. Don't skip lines on your final copy. Put your final copy in your portfolio.

Feel Proud of Your Seven Chapters!

CHAPTER

Dreams of Reaching a Friend

Think of a friend or relative—anyone who has been important to you. You're about to write a personal letter to that person. When you are finished, you can mail your letter if you wish.

Below is the format to follow for a personal letter. You may look at a completed example on page 62.

_____

your street address and apartment number

_____

your city,   state   ZIP code

_____ , _____

today's month   day   , year

Dear _____ ,

first name or nickname

_____

      Indent the first line of each new paragraph one inch from the left margin.

_____

_____

_____

      (You've been writing paragraphs. Have you noticed? You've already written seven chapters of paragraphs. Every time you started a different topic, you began a new paragraph. This time *you* decide when you're changing topics. Then start a new paragraph.)

_____

_____

_____

_____

Writing Your First Draft:

Hint: How long should a paragraph be?

Answer: Three to five sentences is often about right. If your paragraph is over a half-page long, look to see if you changed topics without noticing.

Write your letter below.

_____

_____

_____

_____

_____

_____

_____

_____

_____

_____

_____

_____

_____

Example of a Personal Letter

P.O. Box 8906
Route 77
Riverbend, KY 82503
Feb. 10, 1996

Dear Aunt Carrie,

You'll be surprised to get this letter from me. I haven't written since we moved away from Greenfield.

Yesterday I was going through some boxes of things, and I came across a yellow nightgown you gave me when I spent a week with you. I was eleven or twelve years old.

I remember that visit. You taught me how to milk a cow and gather eggs without getting pecked. I liked sitting by your kitchen stove while you baked biscuits and fried bacon.

Now I'm an aide at Gardenway Nursing Home, and I take classes at our community college. I'm studying to become a records clerk. I'd like to work in the office of a nursing home or hospital.

Danny is stationed at Fort Fullerton. Mama had the flu in January, but now she's recovered. I hope you're well.

Love,
Jenny

Listener's Responses

Now that you've written the practice letter in this chapter, you're ready to review your writing. First, you'll **hear** what you wrote. Then, you'll **revise** it.

To hear how your writing sounds, ask a classmate, friend, or teacher to read it out loud to you, or you could read it aloud to a listener. (Tell the reader to ignore spelling and punctuation for now. You'll fix that later.)

_____

Name of reader or listener

☐ Check Box

Next ask your classmate or friend to write responses to the following statements.

1. Describe what you liked about the way the letter was written.

_____

_____

2. Write a question beginning with *How.*

_____

_____

3. Write a question beginning with *Why.*

_____

_____

4. Please find and underline a sentence you really liked.
    Thank you!

Revising Your Writing:

Consider your listener's responses. You may decide to do any of the following:

- Add information.
- Change words or sentences.
- Rearrange sentences or paragraphs.

Cross out words you want to change. Write revisions on the dotted lines on the practice pages.

Before proofreading, let's review names and titles.

Names and Titles

Capitalize only specific (called **proper**) names of places.

Examples:	**Proper Names**	**General Names**
	Gardenway Nursing Home	a nursing home
	Rivertown Community College	our community college
	Fort Fullerton Air Force Base	an air force base
	Shady Grove Dairy	a dairy

Now it's your turn. Underline the proper names that should be capitalized in these sentences.

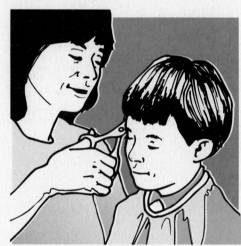

1. I attended george carver middle school.

2. Which middle school did you attend?

3. My grandfather worked for the swanson lumber mill.

4. My stepdad was a pilot at the air force base.

5. My sister is going to beauty school.

6. I'll study helicopter repair at johnson aerial mechanics' college.

Capitalize work titles when they're a part of a specific **(proper)** name.

Examples:	**Proper Names**	**General Names**
	Dr. Alicia Ricardo	my doctor
	President Leonard Cohen	the president
	Dr. Sarah Chan	our dentist
	Lieutenant Reginald Fox	a lieutenant

It's your turn again. Underline the words that should be capitalized.

7. My little brother wants to become a dentist.

8. Our group needs a secretary and a president.

9. I made an appointment with dr. Alonzo.

10. Did you know that many women become sergeants?

Check the answers on page 120. Then check capitalization of the names in your letter. Save these tips in your portfolio for future use.

Lively Letters

General: Dear Good Buddy,
How are you? I'm fine.
. . .hmmmmm. Not very interesting. Try again.

More Specific: Dear Good Buddy,
How are you? I'm frisky.
. . .more interesting this time. Now tell some more.

Very Specific: Dear Good Buddy,
How are you? Since I quit smoking and started bicycling to school, my legs are
like iron. I'm charged with vigor, and Suzi now calls me "Tiger."
Wowee! Now you're seeing a picture!

The word **fine** had such broad meaning, it didn't mean much. The word **frisky** was
more specific. You started seeing something. However, a bicycling tiger with legs of
iron starts your imagination rolling.

Look at another example.

Specific words are more interesting than broad, general words.

General: We had a good time.
What does good mean? Do you have a picture of it?

Specific: We danced until Zolanda's heels broke, and I couldn't straighten my back.
Now you know what kind of time they had!

Now it's your turn.

General: We had a good breakfast.

Write some specific, flavorful, breakfast foods:

_____   _____

_____   _____

Change the general sentence so it describes specific breakfast foods.

_____

Specific words describe a breakfast we can smell, taste, see, and even hear.

Examples: Crisp cereal crunches. Scrapple sizzles. Coffee can perk.

Check the sentence on page 120.

Here's a sentence that's very general.

The kitchen was a mess.

Use your imagination to describe a messy kitchen. Try to use specific words.

List what you would   see   _____

smell   _____

touch   _____

taste   _____

Write a paragraph of related sentences describing a messy kitchen or any other messy room.

_____

Indent an inch.

_____

_____

_____

_____

_____

_____

_____

_____

Did you tell what you saw, heard, felt, and smelled? Ask your teacher to check your sentences when you are finished.

Revising Your Writing:

Go back now and read your letter again. Pretend you are the person who will receive your letter. Read it aloud. Replace general words with specific words. Use your senses to describe.

If you want to add paragraphs, use notebook paper.

Personal Letters

Reread your practice letter. Using the following checklist, complete your final draft.

1. **Check your letter for paragraphing.**

Did you start new paragraphs
when you changed topics? _____

Did you set the first sentence
an inch or more to the right? _____

Mark changes you'll make and initial the box.

☐
Your Initials

2. **Check your paragraphs for run-on
sentences.**
Separate any you find and initial the box.

☐
Your Initials

3. **Check your letter for general words.**
Change them to specific words. Use your
senses to describe. Initial the box.

☐
Your Initials

4. Ask a proofreader to check spelling.
Ask your proofreader to sign here.

_____
Proofreader's signature

5. Show your practice letter to your teacher.
Ask your teacher to initial the box.

☐
Teacher's Initials

Well Done!

Now you're ready to write your final draft.

Writing Your Final Draft:
Use a word processor in your
classroom to write a neat copy of
your letter. Use the spell checker
and then *print two copies.*

or

**Handwrite a neat copy to
mail.** Write on only one side of
the paper. Leave wide margins on
both sides and on the bottom.
Photocopy your letter.

Put your final copy in your portfolio.

Mail the other copy.

Now you're ready to mail your letter.

Address your envelope like the sample shown below.

Be sure to write or print clearly.

your name
apartment and street address
city, state   ZIP code

USA 29

name of friend or relative
apartment number or P.O. Box
street address
city, state   ZIP code

What if you don't know your friend's ZIP code?

Many phone books have pages listing ZIP codes. Look at the table of contents near the front for "ZIP codes."

Post offices have booklets listing ZIP codes. Look on the tables in the lobby or ask a clerk.

Check

□

Notice the comma between city and state.

□

Notice there is *no* comma between state and ZIP code.

□

Notice abbreviations: St., Rd., Ln., Ave., Apt.
    Capitalize the first letter. End with a period.

Personal letters can be shared—
                    saved—
                        reread—
                            and they're cheap!

Getting Results

A **formal letter** often gets the results you need.

Example of a Formal Business Letter

```
                              Apt. 4A
                              1081 Oldbrick St.
                              Packer City, IL 22059
                              Aug. 8, 1996


Mr. Norris Nelson
2306 Harris Way
Packer City, IL   22060

Dear. Mr. Nelson:

    We rent an apartment on the fourth floor of your
building on Oldbrick St. We've lived here for two
years. Yesterday we noticed a broken step in the central
stair. Everyone who lives in this building uses this stair.

    Please send a repair person to replace the broken
step before someone falls. This step is between the
second and the third floors, in the lower part.

    If you have questions, you can phone me at work
during the daytime at 726-2214, or at home in the
evening at 726-0039. We appreciate your attention to this
matter. Thank you.


                              Sincerely,

                              Al LeLoueur
                              Al LeLoueur
```

Formal letters are polite.   They're business-like.

They're business letters.

Writing Your First Draft:

Write your own letter to a landlord. Choose a real or imaginary problem. Request a remedy.

This is the format for your practice formal business letter. Use a pencil so you can erase. You may make up names and addresses. If you need help, look at the example on page 69.

your street address

_____, _____
city,   state   ZIP code

_____, _____
month   day   ,   year

M _____
   landlord's first name   last name

_____
landlord's street address

_____, _____
city,   state   ZIP code

Dear M ___ _____,
              last name only

Tell: who you are,

and why you're writing.

Start a new paragraph when you tell what you're requesting.

Tell exactly what you need.

Tell how you can be reached.

Capitalize the word *Sincerely*.

Sign your first and last names.

Print or type both names underneath.

Listener's Responses

Now that you've written a practice, formal business letter, you're ready to review your writing. First, you'll **hear** what you wrote. Then, you'll **revise** it.

To hear how your writing sounds, ask a classmate, friend, or teacher to read it out loud to you, or you could read it aloud to a listener. (Tell the reader to ignore spelling and punctuation for now. You'll fix that later.)

_____

Name of reader or listener

☐

Check Box

Next ask your classmate or friend to write responses to the following statements.

1. In your own words tell what the renter's problem is.

_____

_____

(If the listener did this correctly, without help, then the letter is clear. If the listener didn't understand, you need to revise your letter.)

2. Did the renter tell:

what needs to be done? _____

where to do it? _____

how to contact the renter if there are questions? _____

3. Did the renter sound polite and reasonable? _____
If the answer is "no," explain what should be changed.

_____

4. If you really were the landlord, what would you do?

_____

Thank you!

Revising Your Writing:
Consider your listener's responses. You may decide to do any of the following:

- Add information.
- Change words or sentences.
- Rearrange sentences or paragraphs.

Cross out words you want to change. Write revisions on the dotted lines on the practice pages.

Before proofreading, let's review salutations and closings.

Salutations and Closings

The way you greet the person you're writing is called the **salutation.**
(Think of a salute.)

In a personal letter, you use a first name and a comma in the salutation.

Example: Dear Anna,

When you write a formal business letter, you use the last name and a colon in the salutation.

Example: Dear Mr. Santiago:

The way you close your letter is called the **closing**. (Logical, huh?)

You can close your personal letter with many different words, a comma, and then your name.

Example:

Write soon,	Fondly,	Best wishes,	Love,	Your friend,
Ashley	Zach	Peggy	Petrea	Louis DeCarlo

We close business letters with the words *Sincerely, Sincerely yours,* or *Yours truly.*

Example:

Sincerely yours,   Yours truly,
Philip Oakley   Joseph Stern

Now it's your turn. Answer the following questions.

1. How will you write the salutation of your formal business letter?

_____

_____

2. What punctuation mark is used after a business letter's salutation?

_____

3. How many *e's* are in **Sincerely**?

_____

4. What punctuation mark is used in the closing of a business or personal letter?

_____

Check the answers on p. 120.

Formal Letter

1. **Paragraphing**
   Did you group your ideas into paragraphs and indent each one? Check your paragraphs and initial the box.

   ☐ Your Initials

2. **Purpose**
   Does the first paragraph tell who you are and why you are writing? _____

   Does another paragraph tell exactly what you're requesting? _____

   When you can say "yes" on both lines, initial the box.

   ☐ Your Initials

3. **Punctuation**
   You should have:

   Checks

   —a comma between city and state ☐

   —nothing between state and ZIP code ☐

   —a comma between day and year ☐

   —a colon after "Dear M___ _____:" ☐

   —a comma after "Sincerely," ☐
   You're a careful writer.

   Great Work!

4. Ask a proofreader to check your spelling.
   Ask your proofreader to sign here.
   _____
   Proofreader's signature

5. Show your practice letter to your teacher.
   Get credit.

   ☐ Credit

Word process a neat copy of your formal letter.

Now you're ready to write your final letter.

or

Handwrite your letter. Blue or black ink is used for hand-written business letters. Write on only one side of the page. Leave wide margins at the bottom, top, and sides of the page.

Put your final copy in your portfolio.

Save this page for future use.

CHAPTER 10

Dreams of Security

In this chapter, you'll write about your dreams of job security.

Writing Your First Draft: Whatever you write is all right. Don't worry about spelling or neatness. Write on only the solid lines so you'll have room to make changes.

What work did you do?

Were you paid?

What did you like

and dislike

about this job?

My first job
_____

What would you like about this job?

What training will you need?

A job I would like to have someday
_____

Maybe you'll get this job. On the next page, see how to request a job interview.

Word Wisdom If you write the word **paid**, spell it like **aid** with a *p* in front.

This is a sample letter requesting an interview for a job. You'll make up your own letter on page 78. Notice as you read that the paragraphs are not indented. This is called **block style**, and it is the most commonly used format in typed letters.

5891 Greenwood St., Apt. 509
Harbor City, MI 02943
May 27, 1997

Personnel Department
Monmouth Tool and Die Making Corporation
42886 Industrial Way
Urbanville, MI 02965

Dear Personnel Director:

I am applying for the position of apprentice tool and die maker, which was advertised by your company in the *City News*.

I am completing my GED at Lewison Community College. While working on my GED, I also took vocational classes in welding and industrial design. I earned an A in welding and a B in design. These classes prepared me to work safely and creatively.

In addition to school work, I have worked part-time for the Eversharp Knife Company. I began working there eighteen months ago. This experience has given me some practical knowledge of tool and die making and has also let me know that this is the type of work I really want for my future career.

Because of my interest and willingness to learn the tool and die making trade, I think that I will be an asset to your company.

I would welcome an opportunity to interview at your convenience. I have enclosed my résumé and can forward references at your request.

Sincerely,

Carlos Escobata

Carlos Escobata

Enclosure

The following letter is another sample of a format you can use when writing your own letter. It is **full-block style**. Either format is fine for business letters.

5891 Greenwood St., Apt. 509
Harbor City, MI 02943
May 27, 1997

Personnel Department
Monmouth Tool and Die Making Corporation
42886 Industrial Way
Urbanville, MI 02965

Dear Personnel Director:

I am applying for the position of apprentice tool and die maker, which was advertised by your company in the *City News*.

I am completing my GED at Lewison Community College. While working on my GED, I also took vocational classes in welding and industrial design. I earned an A in welding and a B in design. These classes prepared me to work safely and creatively.

In addition to school work, I have worked part-time for the Eversharp Knife Company. I began working there eighteen months ago. This experience has given me some practical knowledge of tool and die making and has also let me know that this is the type of work I really want for my future career.

Because of my interest and willingness to learn the tool and die making trade, I think that I will be an asset to your company.

I would welcome an opportunity to interview at your convenience. I have enclosed my résumé and can forward references at your request.

Sincerely,

Carlos Escobata

Carlos Escobata

Enclosure

Keep Writing!

Use the practice page and the prompts below to help you write a letter requesting a job interview. You may write a real letter to a company of interest to you, answer an ad in the newspaper, or make it up.

Your street address _____
Your town, State ZIP code _____
Today's date _____

_____ Name or position of receiver
_____ Name of company or organization
_____ Street address of business
_____ City, State ZIP code
_____ Dear position or name (Mr. or Ms.):

Explain why you're writing. _____
_____

Tell about your training or experience. _____
_____

_____

Explain your interests and hopes. _____

_____

_____

Tell how you can benefit the company. _____

_____

_____

Tell how you can be reached. _____

_____

Sincerely,

Your handwritten signature _____

Typed or printed name underneath _____

_____ Indicate "enclosure" if you enclose a résumé.

Listener's Responses

This job is important to you. Your letter will make a first impression. Be sure your letter sells you!

Ask a listener to pretend to be the person who will receive your letter. Read your letter aloud to this listener. Then ask your listener to answer the following statements.

_____   ☐
Name of reader or listener   Check Box

> **1.** What kind of job does the writer want?
>
> _____
>
> _____
>
> **2.** What experience or training does the writer have?
>
> _____
>
> _____
>
> **3.** How can the writer benefit the company?
>
> _____
>
> _____
>
> **4.** What sort of person does the writer seem to be?
>
> _____
>
> _____
>
> Thank you.

Revising Your Writing:

If your listener didn't remember or understand what you wrote, make your letter clearer.

Add to it.   Change it.   Rearrange it.

Cross out words you want to change. Then write any revisions on the dotted lines on the practice pages.

Before proofreading, let's review business letter punctuation.

Business Letter Punctuation

Check your practice letter.

Capitalize *Rd., St., Ave.*
City **(comma)** State **(no comma)** ZIP
Month **(no comma)** day **(comma)** 199-

Leave four blank lines.
Mr. or Ms. first name and last name
(If you don't know the name, state the position: President, Manager, Personnel Director, etc.)
name of company or agency or business **(capitalize each word)**
street address
city **(comma)** state **(no comma)** ZIP code **(maps in phone books show ZIP codes)**
Leave one blank line.
Dear Mr. or Ms. last name:
Leave one blank line.
Tell why you're writing in the first paragraph.

Tell about your qualifications and interest in another paragraph.

Tell how you can benefit the business and tell how you can be reached. In addition to your own phone number, you might include a message phone number. Ask for an interview.

Sincerely,

Sign your first and last name.

typed or printed name

Enclosure **(if you enclose a résumé)**

Save this form for future use.

Business Letter

What a lot of work! Yes, but a careful business letter can bring big rewards. So, now reread your practice letter and use the checklist below to complete your final letter.

1. Check sentences to be sure they don't run on. Then initial the box.

Your Initials

2. Read aloud from your last to first sentence. Fix incomplete sentences and write your initials in the box.

Your Initials

3. You have already checked paragraphing and punctuation. Yea! Go ahead and initial the box.

Your Initials

4. Because this letter is important, ask two proofreaders to check spelling.

First proofreader's signature

Second proofreader's signature

5. Show your practice letter to your teacher. Ask your teacher to initial the box.

Teacher's Initials

Great Work!

Now you're ready to write your final draft.

Writing Your Final Letter: Leave big margins as you word process your formal business letter.

or

Handwrite a neat copy. If you handwrite your letter, use only blue or black ink.

Keep a copy of this model letter in your portfolio.

The Job of Your Dreams

Résumés:

When you write to request a job interview, you may enclose a résumé. A **résumé** shows your work experience and training. It lets the hiring person see your preparation for the job.

Example of a Résumé

Hillary Nguyen
394 E. 23rd St., Apt. 632
Oceanvista, CA 91509
(503) 748–3321

Responsible, hard-working, and eager to put skills in typing,
word processing, and filing to work in a clerical position.

SKILLS
- Type 50–60 WPM
- Operate WordPerfect
- File both soft and hard copy
- Take precise telephone messages
- Understand and follow office procedures

EXPERIENCE
Position:	Volunteer Office Assistant, January–June 1997
Company:	Poulet Poultry Producers
Address:	1896 Tarragon Rd., Cackling Valley, CA 91510
Supervisor:	Bertha Overtell (503) 747–4501

Position:	Food Server, September, 1994–January, 1996
Company:	Tom's Quick Counter
Address:	806 Main Lane, Oceanvista, CA 91509
Supervisor:	Thomas Park (503) 748–9183

EDUCATION
Keyboard College, Certificate of Achievement, 1997
Oceanside Opportunity School, GED, 1996
Hillcrest Elementary School

References Available Upon Request

Writing the First Draft of Your Résumé: Write your own résumé following this format. It can show your actual experience and training, or the experience you'd like to have.

Write your own practice résumé on this form and follow the pattern shown. Your résumé can show your actual experience and training or it can show the experience you would like to have.

Name _____

Street address _____

City, State ZIP_____

_____

_____

Job Objective _____

_____

_____

_____

Skills _____

_____

_____

_____

_____

_____

_____

Experience _____

_____

_____

_____

_____

_____

_____

_____

_____

Education _____

_____

_____

_____

_____

_____

References Available Upon Request

Résumés

Reread your résumé, using the following checklist.

1. Does it look well-placed on the page? _____

Are all four margins wide enough? _____

Did you leave space between sections? _____
Draw arrows if you'll rearrange.
Then initial the box.

Your Initials

2. Did you capitalize and use a period
if you wrote these abbreviations:
Apt., Rd., St., Ave., S., N., W., or *E.?*
Check these, and then initial the box.

Your Initials

3. Ask a proofreader to check spelling.
Ask your proofreader to sign here.

Proofreader's signature

4. Ask your teacher to check your résumé.
Ask your teacher to initial the box.

Teacher's Initials

Well Done!

Now you're ready to write your final draft.

Résumés are always typed on a typewriter or word processor. Prepare yours now.

In case you are wondering, the word **résumé** has accent marks because it is a French word. When you type it, you may type it without the marks—*resume*.

Once your résumé is factual and correctly prepared, you can take it to a copy shop to have copies made. You will then have them available when you apply for jobs.

Hot Tip: Have your résumé copied on off-white, gray, or tan paper so it will stand out from résumés done on plain white paper. File your master and two or three copies in your portfolio.

Thank You Letters

What if you are interviewed for a job? After the interview, it's a good idea to write a thank you letter.

Example of a Thank You Letter

> 5891 Greenwood St., Apt. 509
> Harbor City, MI 02943
> June 11, 1997
>
> Mr. James Crocker, Personnel Director
> Monmouth Tool and Die Making Corporation
> 42886 Industrial Way
> Urbanville, MI 02965
>
> Dear. Mr. Crocker:
>
> Thank you for taking time to talk with me yesterday. I am interested in finding work that is challenging and rewarding, and this is why I am eager to fill the position of apprentice tool and die maker with your company.
>
> My part-time work at the Eversharp Knife Company has given me good, preparatory experience, and the classes I took at Lewison Community College added to my training. I am well-prepared to apprentice with the Monmouth Corporation.
>
> If there are any other questions that I may answer, please let me know. I look forward to hearing from you soon.
>
> Sincerely,
>
> Carlos Escobata
>
> Carlos Escobata

Writing the First Draft of Your Thank You Letter.

Following the above model, make up your own letter now. Use the guide on the next page. You know the interviewer's last name, so you can use it. The middle paragraph is a good place to remind the interviewer of your strengths.

Word Wisdom

Personnel refers to employees.
Personal means private or individual.

Your street address _____

Your town, state ZIP code _____

Today's date _____

_____ First and last name of interviewer

_____ Capitalized name of company or agency

_____ Street address of business

_____ City, State ZIP code

_____ Dear (Mr. or Ms.) last name only:

In this paragraph thank the interviewer, and remind him/her of your interest in the work.

_____

_____

_____

_____

In this paragraph remind the interviewer of your training, skills, and strengths.

_____

_____

_____

_____

Offer to answer questions. You might give your phone number and a message number.

_____

_____

_____

_____

                              Sincerely,

Your handwritten signature _____

Typed or printed first and last name _____

Listener's Responses

Now that you've written a practice formal thank you letter, you're ready to review your writing. First, you'll **hear** what you wrote. Then, you'll **revise** it.

To hear how your letter sounds, ask a classmate, friend, or teacher to read it out loud to you. Pretend you are the hiring person as you listen to the letter. (Tell the reader to ignore spelling and punctuation for now. You'll fix that later.)

_____

Name of reader

☐ Check Box

Next ask your reader to write responses to the following statements.

1. What impression will the writer's letter make on the hiring person?

_____

_____

_____

2. Describe how the writer can benefit the company.

_____

_____

_____

Thank you!

Revising Your Writing:

Consider your reader's responses. You may decide to:

- Add information.
- Change words or sentences.
- Rearrange sentences or paragraphs.

Cross out words you want to change. Write any revisions on the dotted lines on the practice pages.

Formal Thank You Letters

Reread your practice thank you letter. Use the checklist below to complete your final draft.

1. Check your letter for correct **format**.
Did you leave a wide enough margin
at the top and down the right edge of the paper?
Rearrange your letter if necessary.
Write your initials in the box.

Your Initials

2. Check your letter for correct **punctuation**.
Did you place commas between city and state
but not between state and ZIP code?
Did you use a colon (:) after the greeting?
Did you use a comma (,) after the closing?
Correct your letter if necessary.
Write your initials in the box.

Your Initials

3. Are all sentences:
Complete and independent?
Separated from each other?
Then write your initials in the box.

Your Initials

4. Ask a proofreader to proofread and
sign here.

_____
Proofreader's signature

5. Ask your teacher to check your practice
letter and give credit.

Teacher's Initials

Job Well Done!

Now you're ready to write your final letter.

Writing Your Final Letter:
Use a word processor in your
classroom to write a neat copy of
your letter. Double-space and use
the spelling checker.

or

Handwrite a neat copy.
Write on only one side of the
paper. Leave wide margins on the
bottom, top, and sides of the
paper. Don't skip lines on your
final copy. Use blue or black ink.

Proudly place it in your portfolio.

CHAPTER 12

Memories and Dreams of Love

In this chapter, you'll write about memories and dreams of love.

Writing Your First Draft: Just write! Put your ideas down on the paper. Answer the questions that appear along the side margin. Don't worry about spelling or neatness now. You may skip any topic or change it to one of your own choice.

How old were you?

I had a crush on

Tell about the person, or people, who made your heart beat faster.

Describe your date.

A date I remember

Did you get ready?

Where did you go?

What did you do?

How did you feel?

Word Wisdom If you use the word **beautiful**, notice the *e a u* spelling.

Change any paragraph you wish.

Where did you meet?

I met my spouse (or boyfriend, or girlfriend, or partner)

What was your first impression?

Were you right?

What did you do?

When we were together we

Where did you eat?

What did you like to do with this person?

This gift could be to a friend or a relative.

A gift I remember giving

Did you make it, or buy it?

Keep Writing!

Change any paragraph to fit your own life.

How did you feel about this gift?

A present I remember receiving

What happened to it?

When did you decide?

I decided to marry (or not to marry)

What did each of you say?

How did you feel?

When should people marry?

My thoughts about marriage

Does each person have a role?

What's right for you?

Word Wisdom

If you used the word **received**, notice that it *does* follow the rule, *i* before *e* except after *c*.   **RECEIVED**

You may change any of these paragraphs.

Describe this person.

My best friend (or spouse, or partner) is

_____

_____

_____

Tell about his/her personality.

_____

_____

_____

_____

What makes this person happy and unhappy?

_____

_____

_____

_____

How does this person act?

_____

_____

_____

How is this person like, and unlike, you?

_____

_____

_____

Give a physical description.

_____

_____

_____

How does this person dress?

_____

_____

_____

_____

Writer's Hint:

When you move from personality to physical description, **begin a new paragraph**.
Remember to move the first line on the new paragraph to the right. (If you forgot how to
paragraph, look back at Chapter 8.)

If a baby was born to someone in your family, or a close friend, or yourself, tell about it. When you begin a paragraph, remember to indent the first line about an inch.

Your first paragraph could be about how you learned of the pregnancy.

How did you feel?

What happened at the time of the birth?

Begin a new paragraph if your story moves from one place to another or to another time.

Describe the baby.

Word Wisdom If you write **pregnant**, spell it p r e g n a n t.

Listener's Responses

● ●

Read your Chapter 12 paragraphs aloud to an interested listener.

_____   ☐
Name of listener   Check Box

Ask your listener to respond to the following statements.

1. Describe what you liked about the author's writing.

_____

_____

_____

2. Ask about something the author did not tell.

_____

_____

Use notebook paper if you need more room to write. Skip lines.
Could you use your senses to tell more about the people you described?

People *How did they*	List words to brainstorm. *Look?*	*Sound?*	*Move?*
1. Sonya ___ (name)	sad, frowning, bathrobe, untied shoes, limp hair	unhappy, whiny voice, shuffling sounds, sniffling	slowly tapping fingers
2. ___ (name)			
3. ___ (name)			
4. ___ (name)			

Revising Your Writing:

Consider your listener's reactions. You may decide to do any of the following:
Add.   **Cross out.**   **Change.**   **Rearrange.**

This is your story. Tell it the way you wish.
Before proofreading, let's review some commonly confusing words. Then, check for punctuation and spelling.

More Sneaky Sound-Alikes
new and knew

New describes recent things.

   Examples: a new car   new baby   new idea

Knew means had knowledge. It is the past tense of know. The *k* is silent.

   Examples: You knew that, didn't you?   I knew the answer to her question.

Now it's your turn. Fill in the blanks with the correct word.

1. I _____ what I wanted.

2. I like your _____ shoes.

3. My car is used but it's _____ to me.

4. He tried to hide it, but she _____ what he was up to.

5. The scientist _____ how to invent an unusual tool.

6. Sally tried a _____ recipe.

Check the answers on page 120.

Now make up a sentence for *new* and *knew.*

_____

_____

_____

Can you write a sentence using both words?

_____

_____

_____

Ask your teacher to check these sentences. Then save this page to use in the future.

now and know

Now rhymes with *cow* and means at this time.

> **Example:**   Do it now!

Know means to have knowledge.

> **Examples:**   Do you know what I mean?   **Know** sounds like the word *no*.

CONFUSED?

Just remember! The letter *k* is your clue.
>   *Know* and *knew* are about knowledge and knowing.

Now it's your turn.   Since you know about these words, fill in the blanks with the correct word.

1. I want my dinner _____ !

2. Do you _____ the answer?

3. Do you really _____ when to use these words?

4. Could we please go _____ ?

5. Let's practice right _____ .

6. I _____ this is a tricky business.

Check the answers on page 120.

Make up a sentence for each word.

_____

_____

Ask your teacher to check these sentences.

Reread your paragraphs checking *new, knew, now,* and *know*. Save this page for future use.

Chapter 12

Reread your practice paragraphs using the following checklist.

1. Read your sentences to see if they are separated. Separate all run-on sentences. Write your initials in the box.

Your Initials

2. Read the last sentence, then the next-to-last sentence, then the sentence before that, listening for completeness. Put your initials in the box.

Your Initials

3. See if you started a new paragraph an inch to the right each time your story moved to a new idea. Initial the box.

Your Initials

4. Check for sound-alikes. Did you check the correct spelling of these words? Initial the box.

Your Initials

5. Ask a proofreader to check your spelling. Ask your proofreader to sign here.

Proofreader's signature

6. Show your paragraphs to your teacher. Ask your teacher to initial the box.

Teacher's Initials

Splendid Work!

Now you're ready to write your final draft.

Writing Your Final Draft:
Use a word processor to write a neat copy. Double-space and use the spelling checker.

or

Handwrite a neat copy in ink.
Write on only one side of the paper. Leave wide margins at the bottom, top, and sides of the page.

Put your final copy in your portfolio.

Memories of Moving

You decide when to start new paragraphs this time—probably when you move from one topic to the next. Start the first sentence over to the right about an inch. Your paragraph might be about three to five sentences long. They're usually longer than one sentence and not longer than half a page.

Writing Your First Draft:
Write about a big move or a move as small as from one bedroom to another. Your move might have happened at any age.

How old were you?

When I

Why did you move?

(Remember to paragraph.)

Did others move with you, or did you move alone?

How did you feel about it?

Keep Writing!

Did you leave some things behind?

_____

_____

_____

_____

What did you take with you?

_____

_____

_____

What were your impressions of the new place?

_____

_____

_____

_____

What did you have to get used to?

_____

_____

_____

_____

What did you lose?

_____

_____

_____

What did you gain?

_____

_____

_____

_____

Did you indent each first line about an inch—this much [——————————]?

Ask someone to read to see if you began new paragraphs when you moved to new topics.

Reader's signature _____

Where did you go?

I left (or stayed with) my family when

Describe the place where you lived.

If you stayed at home, tell about living with your family.

(Remember to paragraph.)

Most of us have had "lean" times.

A time when I had very little money was when

How did you economize?

What did you give up?

What did you do for fun?

Revising Your Writing:

If your lab has a tape recorder, or if you have a tape recorder at home, tape a reading of your Chapter 13 paragraphs.

Listen to the tape twice.

After the first hearing, tell what you like.

_____

_____

After the second hearing, tell what you'll add or change.

_____

_____

Writers describing places often tell what they saw, smelled, heard, or felt.

List words that describe the places where you were.

Place	saw	smelled	heard	felt
forest	deer	pine	birds	peaceful

Add as much description as you wish.

Skip lines if you use notebook paper.

Revise until you're satisfied with your practice paragraphs.

Before proofreading, let's review a few more homonyms (sound-alikes).

More Sneaky Sound-Alikes
here and hear

Here shows location. You can remember it because if you put a *w* in front of it, you get **where**—and **here** tells where.

Examples: Yvonne, you can put the files here.
I am going to wait here until Rico returns.

Hear is what happens when you listen.
You can remember it because the word *ear* is in hear.

Examples: I can hear you loud and clear.
Did you hear their new song?

Now it's your turn. Fill in the blanks with the correct word.

1. Can you _____ the music?

2. Put your suitcase right _____ .

Now make up a sentence for each word. Ask your teacher to check your sentences.

Hear _____

Here _____

heard and herd

Circle the **ear** in h**EAR**d.

Example: I heard what you said.
A **herd** is a group of cattle.

Example: The Circle Q has a new herd of steers.

Your turn again.

3. "I'm gonna lasso a _____ of dogies. Giddyap, horse!"

4. He _____ what she whispered to her friend.

Check the answers on page 120.

To complete this review, you may need to look back at pages you saved.

She whispered,

1. "Our _____ hearts beat together to one tune.

2. I _____ you love me.

3. I love you _____ .

4. From _____ on we'll be together. When I first saw you,

5. I _____ you'd be mine."

He exclaimed,

6. "I don't _____ what you're talking about!

7. You're _____ romantic for me.

8. Get up on your _____ feet.

9. I want out of here _____ !

10. I _____ something like this would happen."

11. Is this tale _____ sad?

12. We don't _____ what will happen.

13. But those _____ people are in a confusing situation.

14. How will they _____ what to do next?

Check your answers on page 120 and then throw this silly story away.

Chapter 13

Reread your practice paragraphs. Use the checklist below to complete your final draft.

1. Read your paragraphs to see if they are separated. Separate all run-on sentences. Write your initials in the box.

Your Initials

2. Read from end to beginning, listening to each sentence. When each is independent, write your initials in the box.

Your Initials

3. See that apostrophes are used only where letters are missing or to show possession. Then write your initials in the box.

Your Initials

4. Check for all the sound-alikes you reviewed. Did you check the correct spelling of these words? Initial the box.

Your Initials

5. Ask a proofreader to check your spelling. Ask your proofreader to sign this line.

Proofreader's signature

6. Show your work to your teacher. Ask your teacher to initial the box.

Teacher's Initials

Great Work!

Now you're ready to write your final draft.

Writing Your Final Draft:
You have checked your writing and know it's good. Use a word processor to write a neat copy.

or

Handwrite a neat copy.
Write on only one side of the paper. Remember to leave wide margins. Put your final copy in your portfolio.

Draw maps of house plans if you wish.

14

Today's Dreams

In this chapter, you'll write about the dreams you have today.

Writing Your First Draft: Just write! Put your ideas down on the paper. Answer the questions that appear along the side margin. Don't worry about spelling or neatness now. You may skip any topic or change it to one of your own choice.

What do you do when you get up in the morning?

On a typical weekday I

in the afternoon?

What do you do for dinner?

in the evening?

What do you like to do?

On weekends I

or *have* to do?

Saturday?

Sunday?

Keep Writing!

It's OK to skip paragraphs.

What choices did you have?

A choice I'm glad I have made

Why is this choice best?

Most of us would change some things we did.

Something I would do differently if I could live my life over

How would you change your past?

Why?

What about yourself helps you to get along?

My personal strengths are

Word Wisdom

If you use the word **which**, spell it with an *h* after the *w*.

What do you complain about?

Something that "bugs" me

What makes you angry?

What do you feel good about doing?

Something that gives me satisfaction

Why?

Do you carry a photo in your wallet or have something you save?

A photograph (or letter, or card) I saved shows

What was happening when it was made?

Tape-record your paragraphs, or read them to someone you like. Consider what's good in them. Consider how to improve them.

☐ Check for listening

Before proofreading, let's review a few more homonyms.

coarse and course

Coarse means rough or crude.

   Examples: Your beard feels coarse.   Her words are coarse and vulgar.

The word **course** means a way or sequence of activities.

   Examples: The course of the river runs along that row of trees. (a way)
                This golf course goes around a hill. (a way)
                He's following a course of study. (a sequence)
                Of course, she'll agree! It's in the order of things. (the way it is)

Now it's your turn. Fill in the blanks with the correct word. Remember to use *coarse* for rough or crude and *course* for all other meanings.

1. Our math _____ begins with simple addition.

2. A burlap shirt would feel _____ and scratchy.

3. This race track follows a winding _____ .

4. We must choose a _____ of action.

Check the answers on page 120.

Hoarse means roughness in the voice or throat.

   Example: He shouted at the game until his voice became hoarse.

And you know what a *horse* is!

Make up a sentence for each word.

Coarse _____

Course _____

Hoarse _____

Ask someone to check your sentences and then sign here _____

Save this page to use in the future.

	we're	were	where	wear

We're   *We are* snuggles into *we're*. Right?

> **Example:**   We're right on time.
>   Note: The apostrophe marks where the *a* was squeezed out.

Were tells about being in the past.

> **Example:**   Last summer we were in Oklahoma.
>   Note: No letter is missing, so no apostrophe is needed.

Where tells location.

> **Example:**   Where are you taking me?
>   Note: A way to remember that **where** tells location is to find **here** inside it.

Wear tells what we put on our bodies: boots, rings, sweaters.

> **Example:**   I always wear my raincoat when it's raining.

Now it's your turn. Fill in the blanks with the correct word.

1. When I needed help, you _____ always helpful.

2. I don't know _____ I left my keys.

3. _____ going to play ball.

4. I like to _____ this leather vest.

5. _____ going to the movies.

6. _____ can I buy a used TV.

7. _____ you planning to attend the dance?

Check the answers on page 120. Then make up a sentence for each word.

We're _____

Were _____

Where _____

Wear _____

Ask your teacher to check your sentences.

☐ Teacher's Check

Save these tips and pointers for future use.

Chapter 14

Reread your work. Use the checklist below to complete your final draft.

1. Reread your paragraphs for separation of sentences and correct end punctuation. Write your initials in the box.

Your Initials

2. Read your paragraphs backwards, listening for incomplete sentences. Fix them and write your initials in the box.

Your Initials

3. See that apostrophes show either ownership or where a letter is missing. Then initial the box.

Your Initials

4. Check to make sure you've selected the correct sound-alikes. Initial the box.

Your Initials

5. Ask a proofreader to check your spelling. Ask your proofreader to sign this line.

Proofreader's signature

6. Ask your teacher to check your paragraphs and then initial the box.

Teacher's Initials

Now you're ready to write your final draft.

Writing Your Final Draft:
Using a word processor in your classroom, write a neat copy of your paragraphs. Remember to double-space.

or

Handwrite a neat copy to put in your portfolio.
You've written fourteen chapters for your portfolio!

You're Doing Thorough, Careful Work!

15

Dreams of Tomorrow

In this chapter, you'll write about your dreams for your future.

Writing Your First Draft: Just write! Put your ideas down on the paper. Answer the questions that appear along the side margin. Don't worry about spelling or neatness now. You may skip any topic or change it to one of your own choice.

What dreams entertain your mind?

I like to daydream that I'm

If you could be anyone and do anything, what would you choose?

If I could do anything I like, I'd

If you don't have kids, write about a young person you care about.

I hope my children never have to

Word Wisdom If you use **don't**, put an apostrophe where the o had been in **not**.

Remember that you may change or skip any paragraph.

What should a kid you care about do?	My advice to someone growing up today
—or not do?	
Why?	
Which leaders do you like and dislike?	My political opinions
Which party seems best?	
Why?	
What would you like in your future?	Now I'm hoping

Word Wisdom   If you use the word **college**, spell it with an *e* in the middle.

Keep Writing!

Is religion important to you?

My thoughts about religion are

_____

_____

_____

_____

_____

_____

How do you want people to think of you?

I'd like people to say I'm/was

_____

_____

_____

_____

—to remember you?

_____

_____

_____

_____

_____

_____

Now you add any paragraphs you wish on another piece of paper. This is your own book about yourself.

After you've written your practice paragraphs, what do you do next? _____

That's right. You hear them read aloud.

And after you hear them, what do you do next? _____

Correct. You revise them, which is what you should do now.

Word Wisdom

Believe and **belief** follow the *i* before *e* except after *c* rule.

The *E* at the End

An *e* at the end of a word can be a helpful tip.

Breathe

The final *e* causes the first vowel *e* to say its alphabet name.
So we know this word is - - - - - - -br*eeeeeeee*the.

Examples: I cannot breathe under water.   Breathe deeply.

Breath

Without the final *e*, this word rhymes with *death*.

Examples: Take a breath.   Derek's breath smells minty.

Now it's your turn.   Fill in the blanks with the correct word.

1. He was short of _____ .

2. She'll _____ in your face.

3. I need a _____ of fresh air.

4. Do snails _____ through nostrils?

5. The dying soldier drew his last _____ .

You can tell **clothes** and **cloths** the same way.

Clothes

The *e* at the end of clothes makes the first vowel, *o,* say OH!
So, now you've got something to wear!

Examples: Wear your new clothes.   I hung my clothes in the closet.

Cloths

Without the *e* at the end, we have fabric or rags.

Examples: Jake used cloths to wash his car.   Grandma sewed cloths together to make a quilt.

The E at the End

Now it's your turn. Fill in the blanks with the correct word.

6. Don't wear my good _____ when you hang out with your friends.

7. Wipe up that grease with these _____ .

8. The rescuer jumped into the lake with his _____ on.

9. Carmen tore the material into _____ for bandages.

10. Most of the _____ we wear are made out of cotton.

11. She made a colorful bandanna out of varied _____ .

Now choose from *breathe, breath, clothes,* and *cloths.*

12. My _____ are so tight that I cannot

13. _____ .

14. His _____ made mist on the glass.

15. He wiped the spilled milk off with _____ .

Check the answers on page 120.

Save all your tips and pointers for future reference.

Chapter 15

You write the checklist this time. You may peek back at the old ones.

1. _____ ☐
   _____

2. _____ ☐
   _____

3. _____ ☐
   _____

4. _____ ☐
   _____

5. _____ ☐
   _____

After you're out of school, you won't ask a teacher to check your work, but you can check your writing yourself to be sure it's good.

Well Done!

You've Done an Outstanding Job!

Writing Your Final Draft:
Use a word processor in your classroom to write a neat copy of your paragraphs. Double-space and use the spelling check.

or

Handwrite a neat copy.
Write only on one side of the paper. Leave wide margins at the bottom, top, and sides.

Put your final copy in your portfolio.

Save the next page.

CONGRATULATIONS!

You have learned a writing process you can use whenever you need to write clearly and correctly. You can follow this process to achieve good writing for the rest of your life. This process involves the following steps:

1. Gather ideas.

2. Quickly write a first draft.
   a. Skip lines so you can add and change words and sentences.
   b. Don't worry about spelling and punctuation so you can focus on what you're saying.

3. Listen to your writing while someone reads it aloud to you. If you prefer, you can also read it aloud yourself.

4. Revise it.
   Add. Take out. Change. Rearrange.

5. Check your sentences and paragraphs.

6. Have someone else proofread for spelling errors.

7. Write a final version in ink or on a word processor. Remember to use the spelling checker!

Good luck with your writing!

Enjoy successful writing!

Use this page through future years.

You've written about your memories and your dreams. They're important. Your children, or someone who cares about you, may want to save your book. Consider having copies made at a copy shop.

If you want to tell about more, add paragraphs! Decorate with drawings and photos, certificates, invitations, or any flat souvenirs.

You have many more writing skills now than you had when you began, so you'll probably see corrections you want to make. Changes are easy using a word processor. If you are handwriting changes, you don't have to start over whenever you goof. Just draw a neat line through mistakes.

You've completed a big project and written a book to be proud of—a book to save.

Answer Key

Run-On Sentences, p. 8
1. I want my money back. This toy broke the first time we used it.
2. His pickup truck backfired and stopped. He checked all the gauges.
3. We love to dance. We can do country swing, ballroom, and square dancing.
4. Shirley and I went to the beach. We took a bag of sandwiches. The kids came, too.

End Punctuation, p. 9
1. Please explain this to her.
2. I think she needs to know the truth.
3. What a weasel he is!
4. Why does he treat her that way?
5. Does she know what he is like?
6. Do you believe him?
7. Get lost!

Incomplete Sentences, p. 14
1. I was thinking of you.
2. A tree fell on top of the house.
3. The class was delayed because he was late.
4. The children left the party screaming and laughing.

Two/Too/To, p. 15
1. too
2. Too
3. too
4. two
5. too
6. two

Our/Are, p. 22
1. our
2. are
3. are
4. Our
5. Our
6. are

They're/Their/There, p. 23
1. their
2. They're
3. there
4. There

Sample sentences:
They're very kind people.
I babysit for their children.
Please wait over there.
They're going to wait for their friends over there.

Apostrophes, p. 32
Sample uses of the apostrophe:
Don't go near the lake today.
Craig's car is in the garage being repaired.

Apostrophes, p. 33
1. Louis won't listen to me.
2. That's my bus pass.
3. Sally's dog bit someone.
4. Correct.
5. Correct.

Reasons for answers above:
The first three sentences show that a letter is missing or show ownership. The last two show plural nouns.

You're/Your/It's/Its, pp. 34–35
1. You're
2. your
3. your
4. You're

Sample sentences:
You're doing very well in this class.
Do you have your homework?
5. its
6. It's
7. it's
8. Its
9. your
10. You're
11. your
12. your

Threw/Through, p. 41
1. threw
2. through
3. through
4. through
5. threw
6. through

Sample sentences:
I threw a pebble into the lake.
Carlo carried the box through the hallway.

Quit/Quiet/Quite, p. 42
1. quiet
2. quit
3. quite
4. quite
5. quiet
6. Quit
7. quite
8. quit
9. quiet
10. quite

Than/Then, p. 43
1. than
2. Then
3. than
4. then
5. than
6. then

Sample sentences:
I like chocolate better than any other dessert.
When I finish cleaning the house, then we'll go to the park.

Bye/Buy/By, p. 49
1. by
2. buy
3. by
4. Good-bye
5. by

Review, p. 50
Run-On Sentences

We were sitting in the balcony. I heard him start to laugh.
I was waiting to see what would happen next.
1. I'm
2. Don't
3. That's, Gary's
4. correct
5. You're
6. Your
7. They're
8. It's

Break/Brake, p. 57
1. brake
2. break

3. break
4. brake
Sample sentences:
If he is not careful driving his motorcycle, he will break his neck.
The brake on the bicycle did not work.

Whole/Hole, p. 58
1. whole
2. hole
3. no apostrophes
4. won't
Sample sentences:
I won't go to the party with them.
I want to buy a new pair of shoes.

Names/Titles, p. 64
1. George Carver Middle School
2. correct
3. Swanson Lumber Mill
4. correct
5. correct
6. Johnson Aerial Mechanics' College
7. correct
8. correct
9. Dr.
10. correct

Lively Letters, p. 65
Sample sentence:
We had cold orange juice, spicy sausage, and cheese omelettes for breakfast.

Salutations/Closings, p. 73
1. Answers will vary.
   Sample answers:
   Dear Dr. Brady:
   Dear Mr. Ross:
   Dear Ms. Kinsley:
2. The colon (:)
3. two
4. The comma (,)

New/Knew, p. 95
1. knew
2. new
3. new
4. knew
5. knew
6. new

Sample sentences:
I have a new dress to wear to the party.
I knew the answers to all the questions.
I knew the name of the new teacher.

Now/Know, p. 96
1. now
2. know
3. know
4. now
5. now
6. know
Sample sentences:
I am going to leave now.
The children know how to make stew for dinner.

Hear/Here, p. 102
1. hear
2. here
Sample Sentences:
I cannot hear very well.
Please stand over here.
3. herd
4. heard

Review, p. 103
1. two
2. know
3. too
4. now
5. knew
6. know
7. too
8. two
9. now
10. knew
11. too
12. know
13. two
14. know

Course/Coarse p. 108
1. course
2. coarse
3. course
4. course
Sample sentences:
I didn't like the movie because of all the coarse language.
Daniel's favorite course is math.
Jenny has had a hoarse throat for weeks now.

We're/Were/Where/Wear, p. 109
1. were
2. where
3. We're
4. wear
5. We're
6. Where
7. Were
Sample sentences:
We're very happy with our new car.
Yesterday, John and Maria were visiting friends.
Where did you find my keys?
She likes to wear her blue scarf.

Breathe/Breath, pp. 114–115
1. breath
2. breathe
3. breath
4. breathe
5. breath
6. clothes
7. cloths
8. clothes
9. cloths
10. clothes
11. cloths
12. clothes
13. breathe
14. breath
15. cloths